Think About...

30 Days to Transform Your Thinking

by Sisters Forward

Copyright © 2022 by Cassia Elder

All rights reserved. No part of this work may be reproduced, stored in a retrieval system, or transmitted in any form or by any means—for example, electronic, photocopy, recording—without the prior written permission of the author. The only exception is brief quotations in printed reviews.

Printed in the United States of America

Scripture marked (NASB): New American Standard Bible Copyright © 1960, 1971, 1977, 1995, 2020 by The Lockman Foundation, La Habra, Calif.

Scripture marked (CEV): Contemporary English Version, Second Edition (CEV®) © 2006 American Bible Society. All rights reserved.

Scripture marked (NIV): The Holy Bible, New International Version®, NIV®. Copyright © 1973, 1978, 1984, 2011 by Biblica, Inc.® Used by permission. All rights reserved worldwide.

Scripture marked (ESV): The Holy Bible, English Standard Version. Copyright © 2001 by Crossway Bibles, a publishing ministry of Good News Publishers. Text Edition: 2016. All rights reserved.

Scripture marked (MSG): *The Message*. Copyright © 1993, 1994, 1995, 1996, 2000, 2001, 2002. Used by permission of NavPress Publishing Group.

Scripture marked (NLT): The *Holy Bible,* New Living Translation. Copyright © 1996, 2004, 2015 by Tyndale House Foundation. Used by permission of Tyndale House Publishers, Inc., Carol Stream, Illinois 60188. All rights reserved.

Scripture marked (NKJV): New King James Version®. Copyright © 1982 by Thomas Nelson. Used by permission. All rights reserved.

Scriptures marked (AMP): Amplified Bible Copyright © 2015 by The Lockman Foundation. All rights reserved www.lockman.org

Contents

1. Choose Your Thoughts- *Cassia Elder* 5
2. Something to Think About- *Sandi Baete* 8
3. A Greater Plan- *Stephanie Heitz* 11
4. God's Love is True- *Angie Baughman* 14
5. Speaking Truly- *Katie Mason* 17
6. Not 'So,' But 'But'- *Sheri Trusty* 20
7. Honor Me in Your Sorrow- *Teresa Davis* 23
8. Bought with a Price- *Cassia Elder* 26
9. The Honorable Life- *Sandi Baete* 29
10. Humming Birdbrain- *Sheri Trusty* 32
11. Right vs. Wrong- *Teresa Davis* 35
12. What is Right- *Katie Mason* 38
13. Waiting on the Lord- *Stephanie Heitz* 41
14. Indicator Lights- *Sheri Trusty* 44
15. What is a Pure Heart?- *Katie Mason* 47
16. Who God Says You Are- *Cassia Elder* 50
17. Beyond Beautiful- *Sandi Baete* 53
18. Vengeance is Mine- *Teresa Davis* 56
19. Trusting God with My Trouble- *Angie Baughman* 59
20. The Good Reports- *Sheri Trusty* 62
21. Think Commendable- *Cassia Elder* 65
22. Holy Shoddy is Still Shoddy- *Katie Mason* 68
23. Simply Excellent- *Sandi Baete* 71
24. One, Single Mind- *Sheri Trusty* 74
25. Praise Him When It Hurts- *Teresa Davis* 77
26. Joyous Praise- *Angie Baughman* 80
27. What Do You See?- *Sandi Baete* 83
28. Why We Break a Pattern- *Katie Mason* 86
29. The Mind is the Battlefield- *Teresa Davis* 89
30. Change Your Life- *Cassia Elder* 92

Meet Our Contributors & Mission Partner 95

"Finally, brothers *and sisters,*

whatever is *true,*

whatever is *honorable,*

whatever is *right,*

whatever is *pure,*

whatever is *lovely,*

whatever is *commendable,*

if there is any *excellence* and

if anything *worthy of praise,*

think about these things."

Philippians 4:8 (NASB)

1. Choose Your Thoughts

by Cassia Elder

"Finally, brothers and sisters, whatever is true, whatever is honorable, whatever is right, whatever is pure, whatever is lovely, whatever is commendable, if there is any excellence and if anything worthy of praise, think about these things." Philippians 4:8 (NASB)

In his letter to the Philippian church, the Apostle Paul presented us with an astonishing truth: we have control over the thoughts that enter and linger in our minds.

Maybe this truth is not a surprise to you, but not so long ago, the concept that I could choose my thoughts was news to me. For so many years, I had passively entertained every idea that popped into my mind without any consideration as to whether or not it belonged there.

Paul appealed to us from a place of relationship. As part of the family of God, his brothers and sisters in Christ, he instructed us on the types of thoughts that we should think. These words came on the heels of telling us not to be anxious and are a continuation of what to do instead.

Yes, we can choose our thoughts. Choosing well means we should identify and intentionally select the desirable thoughts that Paul listed above. But the opposite is also applicable; we need to identify and intentionally reject undesirable thoughts.

"We demolish arguments and every pretension that sets itself up against the knowledge of God, and we take captive every thought to make it obedient to Christ." 2 Corinthians 10:5 (NIV)

In order to make our thoughts obedient to Christ, we must recognize and remove those things that are contrary to the wisdom and doctrine of God. Then, we are able to replace in our minds thinking that is in alignment with God's thoughts.

Choosing our thoughts well is not automatic. It is a practice that requires self-discipline. The good news is self-discipline is a Fruit of the Spirit. That means it is not something we have to muster up on our own. The Holy Spirit produces the fruit, and we can partner with Him to develop it until it becomes our natural response.

By the power of the Holy Spirit, we can take our thoughts captive.

> Choose true and refuse lies.
>
> Choose honorable and refuse immoral.
>
> Choose right and refuse wrong.
>
> Choose pure and refuse corrupt.
>
> Choose lovely and refuse ugly.
>
> Choose commendable and refuse contemptible.
>
> Choose excellence and refuse mediocrity.
>
> Choose praise and refuse criticism.

I encourage you to revisit that choose/refuse list again and again. Read it out loud. Make it a declaration over your mind and over your life. "Today, I choose true and refuse lies. I choose honorable and refuse…"

As we journey through these devotions together, we will learn strategies to combat the thoughts that do not have the right to take up space in our minds. But that's not all. We will also discover how to intentionally choose the thoughts that strengthen our hearts and honor God.

Let's link arms and determine together to *think about these things*.

Reflection:

To what degree do I allow wrong thoughts to take up space in my mind unchallenged?

How well/often do I intentionally choose to think God-honoring thoughts?

Prayer:

Father God, thank You for the truth that, by the power of Your Holy Spirit living in me, I can choose the thoughts that get to take up space in my mind. Convict me when I allow wrong thoughts to remain for too long, and compel me to choose thoughts that edify me and honor You. In Jesus' name, amen.

2. Something to Think About

by Sandi Baete

"Set your minds on things above, not on earthly things." Colossians 3:2 (NIV)

I have this weird thing that I do. Well, that makes it sound like I only do one weird thing, and that's not even close to the truth. Let's start over. Today I'm going to tell you about one weird habit I have. That's better. I don't recall when this started, but I do know it's not a new behavior. I think it happened randomly once, and, after that, I began to look for ways to intentionally incorporate it into my life. Hopefully, by now you're curious, but it's just as likely you're annoyed with my long introduction to my weird habit, so I'll get to the point.

When I hear a song that isn't of the Christian genre, I listen to the lyrics and try to find a connection between the words and how they relate to Christ and my relationship with Him, even when that isn't the purpose of the song. Love songs are easy to do this with, but I see connections in all types of music. Sometimes changing just one word changes the meaning of the entire song. One "call" away becomes one "prayer" away and suddenly, for me at least, it's about God. Often, no change is needed. The song points to the Lord so clearly for me even when that obviously wasn't the aim of the songwriter. I do this with books and movies, too. No matter the topic or category, I engage with the expectation of the Lord meeting me there. And more often than not, He does.

How's that for weird? I've never heard of anyone else doing this, so I assume it's not a common practice. Of course, I eat cake and ice cream with a fork and thought that was how everyone ate it until recently, so my behavior may not be the best indicator of what's "normal" or "weird". Moving on.

Colossians 3:2 tells us to, "Set your minds on things above, not on earthly things." In other words, we are to think more about heavenly things than earthly things. What a beautiful idea. That is, until we have to face the reality of everyday life here on Earth: jobs to go to, families to care for, and all the other stuff that makes up our days. With so many earthly matters vying for our attention, how do we set our minds on things above?

Consistent Bible study, prayer, fellowship with other believers, and worship are certainly important. But even at our best, these things will not make up the bulk of our day. What if we begin to examine the earthly things and attempt to understand them through the lens of the Kingdom to come? To think about heavenly things as we encounter the earthly things. In this way, we can begin to set our minds on things above, as Scripture instructs.

I'm going to suggest a simple way to help us do this and it comes straight from the focus of our entire devotional, Philippians 4:8. In any circumstance, we can ask ourselves what is true, or noble, or right, or pure, or lovely, or admirable, or excellent, or praiseworthy about this situation? In other words, how do we see God and how should we respond? The answers will be different for each of us, but the questions remain the same because the Lord is in our everyday, no matter what that looks like. He is at our jobs and our dinner tables. He is in the music we listen to, the books we read, the movies we watch. Even when they aren't created with Him in mind. As Romans 11:36 declares, "For from Him and through Him and for Him are all things. To him be the glory forever! Amen." And that's definitely something to think about.

Reflection:

When I set my mind on things above, I can see earthly things in a different way, His way.

How can I practice setting my mind on things above?

Prayer:

Lord, the more I am with You the easier it becomes to think of the world, to come and see things on Earth from Your perspective. Help me to grow in my love for You, spend more time with You, and joyfully anticipate the day I'll be with you in Heaven. In Jesus' name, amen.

3. A greater Plan

by Stephanie Heitz

"Do not be anxious about anything, but in everything by prayer and petition, with thanksgiving, present your requests to God, and the peace that passes understanding will guard your hearts and minds in Christ Jesus." Philippians 4:6-7 (NIV)

I grew up in church listening to the gospel every single Sunday. I even attended a grade school that required a dull, plaid uniform and religion class was part of our daily curriculum. If you asked me if I believed that Jesus is the Son of God who died on the cross to take our sins away and rose from the dead, I would have answered with a resounding, "Yes," but was I truly saved?

I had no concept of God's grace, and I had been working overtime trying to earn God's favor while making all sorts of empty promises to Him in the process.

My relationship status with the Lord was pretty shallow, too. Prayer time consisted of asking Him for everything to go my way, followed by a quick chant of The Lord's Prayer. By no means did I have a grasp of what a lifestyle in Christ looked like.

It wasn't until years later, when I was a young mother, that I would experience the transforming power of stepping into a saving relationship with Jesus Christ.

My husband and I were very happily married and the proud parents of a beautiful, little girl who was just a few months past her first birthday. So many wonderful things were taking place in this magical season of our lives. We were taken by surprise when we found out our family of three would soon be growing. Baby number two was on the way!

Excited to celebrate our good news, we packed up for Northern Ohio and ventured out to visit my husband's family. Only a few days into the trip, I began experiencing cramps and spotting that frightened me. I remember dropping to my knees and begging God, "Please don't let this be happening to me," as I quickly recited an Our Father.

I placed a phone call to my OB/GYN, who happens to be a sold-out Christian and an incredible example of what it looks like to follow Jesus. I explained my symptoms and waited eagerly to hear his medical advice. To my shock, he offered me encouragement from God's Love Letter instead. He advised me to look up Philippians 4:6-7 and gently instructed me to spend some time with the Lord. I quickly ran and grabbed my husband's parents' family Bible and drank in every word of the passage. Once again, I dropped to my knees. But this time, I prayed from the overflow of my heart, and something felt different. A sense of calm came over me like I had never encountered before. I was truly surrendering to God's plan and I knew that whatever the outcome, it was all going to be okay.

Although I shed many tears as I walked through the sadness of a miscarriage, the peace that swept over me that day never left my side. I embraced a living hope like I never had before as I started my journey of trusting in God's provision and greater plan.

Through the loss of one life, who was instantly called home to Heaven, I gained my own life in Christ. I remain eternally grateful that this is part of my story.

Reflection:

Am I continually fixing my mind on Jesus, the Author and Perfecter of my faith, and trusting Him as my provider?

Prayer:

Giver of life, You tell us to trust in You with all of our heart and never lean on our own understanding. We know You have good plans for us and our hope is in You and You alone. In Jesus' name, amen.

4. God's Love is True

by Angie Baughman

"God is love." 1 John 4:8b (NASB)

In the summer of 2010, the minivan carrying our family of four crashed head-on into another vehicle. The other driver had fallen asleep at the wheel, and he crossed the centerline. It was the beginning of a long, painful season for our family, filled with the medical procedures to help heal our bodies and time with the Lord to help heal our souls.

While God ministered to me in my physical brokenness, He also stirred a yearning in me to allow Him to minister to my emotional brokenness. As I dealt with the pain of physical limitations, God invited me to look at the emotional limitations present in my life because I was trying to love Him without truly knowing His love for me.

Because of abuse in my past, I had believed the lie of the enemy that I was not loveable. I thought I was wrong at the core, and I had fallen into a habit of producing, performing, and striving for perfection that gained me affirmation for a moment but didn't last. I searched for love and approval through doing, and when all the doing came to a screeching halt following the car crash, I had to examine what was true.

God's love is true. God is love, and God loves us. He created us and calls us into a relationship with Him because He loves us. Nothing we do and nothing done to us can alter or diminish God's passionate, relentless love for us.

But we have a choice. We can choose to align our thinking with God's love for us, or we can choose to align our thinking with the world's demands to do more, attain more, and be more to make ourselves loveable.

If you struggle to remember God's deep, personal love for you, I encourage you to put together a toolbox of resources you can use to realign your thinking with the truth of God's love. Perhaps personalize one of the tools I use like:

- Select a Scripture or two and put them in a reminder app that's easy to locate on your phone. I love Jeremiah 31:3, which says God loves us with an everlasting love, and Zephaniah 3:17, which says His love renews us.

- Make a playlist of songs that sing God's love over you that you can play when you are doubting the truth of being loved by God.

- Practice a breathing exercise that slows down your internal conversation. I use a simple technique to breathe in slowly, saying, "I am," hold for seven counts, then breathe out slowly, saying "loved." I am... pause... loved. I repeat this four times before thinking again about whatever thoughts were swirling in my mind.

Thinking on the truth of God's love will likely not come easily. But believing the lies of the enemy and striving to attain love isn't easy, either. We can win this mind-war when we intentionally connect ourselves to Christ. An abiding relationship with Him promises to bring an abundance of all we need to live truthfully with God, others, and ourselves.

Reflection:

When my thoughts lead me to believe I am not worthy of love, what will I do to remind myself of God's passionate, unconditional love for me, His beloved child?

Prayer:

Holy Father, You are faithful, loving, and kind. I confess I often run from the love You offer while trying to find love where I will never find it. Thank You for continuing to be merciful and steady. Help me receive Your love. In Jesus' name, amen.

5. Speaking Truly

by Katie Mason

"For the word of the Lord is right and true; He is faithful in all He does." Psalm 33:4 (NIV)

I have a friend who is always quick to offer help whenever a need presents itself. This is a noble and good quality. However, it is partnered with a need for other people to like her. These two qualities together leave my friend so overwhelmed with opportunities to help others that she rarely, if ever, has space to pursue what brings her life joy. Sound familiar? Maybe my friend is you. I know that it is sometimes me.

As believers in Christ, we are confronted with infinite possibilities to help others. We are even commanded to help others. The Bible tells us in Galatians 6:2 that we are to "carry each other's burdens, and in this way you will fulfill the law of Christ." The concept of walking with another believer through their pain is one of the defining tenets of our faith. But what happens when we are so busy walking with others that we neglect our own walk? We do not leave time for Jesus to meet with us and work on our hearts. If we are carrying someone else's burden as a way of denying our own, that is just as much a sin as denying we need Jesus to save us.

We are also told by Jesus to let our "yeses" be "yeses" and our "nos" be "nos." (Matthew 5:7) That is really hard to do. Especially when we are saying "no". It feels like "no" needs a qualifier, doesn't it? As if saying no to someone is not enough of an answer. However, the word no is a complete sentence. Far too often, we forget that. Maybe it's because of our upbringing or societal pressure. As women, it is often hard for us to say no because we are discouraged from doing so. We don't want to disappoint anyone. It's easy for us to find a reason to say yes because that's what we believe is expected of us.

When the Lord speaks to anyone in the Bible, He very rarely gives a qualifier for His answers. God simply commands the person or people to do something and the people or person have the choice to obey. God is always clear on what the consequences will be based on their choice. I know we are not God, but we do have the authority of the Holy Spirit to speak and act on His behalf. That is why we need to be confident in both our yeses and our nos. When we speak to others, we are speaking as representatives of God to them. When God is speaking truly, without waffling, that is our example of how to speak with others.

There are many times when we may need to ask for grace because we said "no" when we should have said "yes". There are even more times when we need to ask for forgiveness when we said "yes" when we should have said "no". Let us each be bold enough to speak truly to the world with the confidence that we are being led by the Holy Spirit in the decisions we make to act or say something. This world would be a much less confusing place if we were speaking truly like our God speaks to us.

Reflection:

Do I need to repent of not speaking truly? Of not letting my yes be yes, and my no be no?

Prayer:

Holy Spirit, direct my mouth to only speak what is true. To not be bogged down in gossip or to speak quickly without considering the impact of my words. Father, please teach me how to speak like You, with both truth and love. In Jesus' name, amen.

6. Not 'So', But 'But'

by Sheri Trusty

"But thou, O Lord, art a God full of compassion, and gracious, longsuffering, and plenteous in mercy and **truth**." Psalm 86:15 (NKJV)

David lived a complex life. When he was a boy, his powerful faith inspired him to sling a stone to slay a giant that grown men were afraid to fight. Then, as an adult, he was unable to conquer his own passions, and he cowardly killed an innocent man so he could take his wife. David was revered as a wise and godly king, but he was also forced into seclusion by those who wanted to steal his reign.

David wrote Psalm 86 as a prayer for seasons of affliction. It was not penned in response to a specific event in his life, but it is a prayer that he could – and that we can – breathe upward to God in seasons of struggle. The prayer encompasses the scope of his lifetime troubles. He acknowledged the destitute condition of his heart in verse one when he told God, "I am poor and needy," and he described his enemies' brutality in verse 14. He said that proud men and violent men were trying to destroy his soul.

Have you been there? Have you been overwhelmed by your neediness as you face the demands of life and Heaven? Have you felt the pressure of your own enemies, the ones who replace swords with the tactics of vicious words and ugly lies? We each have our own verse 14 that describes the pain our enemies have inflicted on us. Our own verse 15 would likely begin with the word, "So." So, God should make them suffer. So, I have the right to be vengeful. So, I can sit and wallow in self-soothing.

Yet, David didn't say, "So." David said, "But." He said, "But You are."

Despite his destructive choices, David developed such a deep love for God that God called him, "a man after His own heart" (I Samuel 13:14). David was able to grasp the truth that his own ungodliness was insurmountable and the only hope he had was in the mercy of God. He understood that he had nothing to offer God but failure, but he knew God joyfully replaces our depravity with His own purity. David was still a mess, but God saw him and treated him as if he were perfect, just like He does for us.

Because David understood God's heart so well and longed so desperately to know more of it, he wasn't overwhelmed when his enemies pursued him with pride and violence. David didn't sit, like we often do, and dwell on the angst and the unknowns. Instead, he regarded truth.

In verse 14, David described his enemies and their schemes, and in verse 15, he immediately switched to acknowledging the truth of God's character. His thoughts were first centered on his enemies, but they didn't run rampant from there, flipping back and forth from fear to despair to anger. Instead, his thoughts immediately jumped from his enemies' malice to the goodness of God. He responded to his crazy, painful circumstances by thinking about the stability of God's character. "But You, Lord, are," David says, compassionate, gracious, slow to anger, merciful, and full of truth.

"Truth" in this verse means what God says is true, but the original Hebrew definition also adds the element of "stability" to the meaning. When we put our trust in what God says is true, our hearts can be calm in seasons of affliction and moments of despair, and we can recognize that our lives, protected in His hands, aren't just flailing in the wind like we thought.

When our enemies push us into a place of fear and sadness, we can dwell on the truth of God's goodness. Thoughts of God's character can settle our hearts and stabilize our souls.

Reflection:

Do my thoughts freeflow in response to my enemies' cruelty?

How can the stability of God's character lead to a stability of heart?

Prayer:

Lord, when I am overwhelmed by life, help my 'so' turn into 'but,' and let my thoughts turn to You and Your unending goodness. In Jesus' name, amen.

7. Honor Me in Your Sorrow

by Teresa Davis

"And call on me in the day of trouble; I will rescue you, and you shall honor and glorify me." Psalm 50:15 (AMP)

How do we honor God in our sorrow? When we suffer in this life, the first thought we usually have is "How do I survive? How am I going to get through this?" It likely is not, "How can I bring honor and glory to God?" The emotion and devastation that ensues set us up for a fall into a deep pit of despair.

There was a man named Job who lived in the land of Uz. He was blameless, a man of complete integrity. Yet, with his suffering, he cursed the day he was born. "I have no peace, no quietness. I have no rest; only trouble comes." Job 3:26 (NLT) The hard part of suffering is a missing timestamp of when it will end. Perhaps Job's despair is relatable to your circumstances.

We try to figure it all out in our own strength. Just like Job, our minds struggle to make sense of it all. For 37 chapters, Job and his friends discussed the why while God listened. In your despair, do you wonder if anyone is listening? Take heart, my friend. If Job was considered blameless yet he struggled in the human condition and God listened, He is listening to you as well. God responded to Job in chapter 38. Communication requires speaking and listening. Are you listening?

In all of Job's suffering, he never stopped communicating with his God. We often think of prayer as a time we set aside to speak our praise and bring our requests. While this is true, prayer also is lament. When life doesn't turn out like we expect, God wants to hear our hearts. Sincere lament laced with anguish is a heart calling out to God in the day of trouble. His own Son prayed in great distress and asked God to remove the suffering that lay before Him. In response, God sent an angel to comfort and strengthen Him.

Perhaps you're thinking, where's my angel? We have something better than an angel; He's called the Holy Spirit. If you have asked Jesus to be the Lord of your life, confessed your sins, and committed your life to serve Him, the Holy Spirit dwells within you. In fact, we are told His presence will never leave us or forsake us. (Hebrews 13:5)

Often, disappointment sets in when we don't get the answer we've waited and longed for. Rescue doesn't always look like we expect. Jesus asked for the suffering to be removed, but the answer was no. He was grieved just like us, and God was compassionate toward Him and sent comfort and strength for the journey ahead. Job suffered in spite of his reputation with God, yet God listened as he poured out his heart of lament and restored twice as much for what he had lost.

We honor God with our sorrow when we continue to seek Him in the depths of our pain. When we cry out to Him and seek answers in His Word, the Holy Spirit will bring comfort.

"Call to me, and I will answer and show you great and unsearchable things you do not know." Jeremiah 33:3 (NIV)

Reflection:
How will I communicate my pain and sorrow to God today?

As I seek Him in His Word, how will I prepare myself to wait and listen for Him to show me great and unsearchable things?

Prayer:
Father, please hear my prayer as I pour out my lament and disappointments to You. Send comfort and strength for the journey and reveal Yourself to me in ways I could have never imagined. In Jesus' name, amen.

8. Bought with a Price

by Cassia Elder

"Love one another with brotherly affection. Outdo one another in showing honor." Romans 12:10 (ESV)

In the key verse above, "one another" refers to our fellow believers. Paul wanted to remind us that those of us in Christ are all related by the blood of Jesus. And as brothers and sisters, we should be devoted to each other with the genuine, unique, divine love shared between members of God's family.

The New International Version translates the second half of this verse, "Honor one another above yourselves." That sure is counter to the message of our culture that tells us to seek our own honor above all else and to only respect those who show us respect. But God invites us to step away from the world's toxic ideology of self-focus and to instead focus on loving others. This means we think less about our own honor and constantly consider how we can honor our brothers and sisters.

Do you own anything especially valuable? How do you treat, handle, and care for that item? For Christmas last year, my husband bought me a sparkly, rose gold wristwatch with a designer name brand engraved on the face. I don't wear it to mow the lawn or dig in the garden or go to the gym. This timepiece is only worn when the occasion and activity give me reasonable assurance that it won't get dirty, sweaty, or banged up. When the evening comes to a close, I always store it in the original jewelry box. Because my husband's gift is precious, both due to the price tag and out of sentimentality, I attend to it with the utmost regard.

The word translated "honor" in our key verse means to value, price, pay respect, and perceive worth. Interestingly, this is the same word used in 1 Corinthians 6:20 where Paul said, "You were bought with a *price*." He was talking about how we believers have been paid for with the shed blood of the sinless Messiah. Showing honor means recognizing that the acquisition of each of our spiritual siblings was the most expensive purchase ever made.

The way we think about our brothers and sisters in Christ, the way we esteem them and interact with them, should be through the same lens with which God sees them—the costly crucifixion of His only Son. Every child of God is of high value, bought with a great price, deserving much honor.

So, this is the point in a conversation where we usually want to put in a caveat. "I honor others if…" The thing is, Scripture doesn't give us qualifiers that allow us to only love *if* others meet our chosen criteria. You see, honor is not contingent on our perception of the other person's honorability; it is based on the command that we be people of honor who treat others accordingly. Even if we don't like their ideology or doctrine or politics—we can disagree while still showing the respect due the sacrifice of our Savior who covers all of our sins.

When Paul said to "*Outdo* one another in showing honor," he urged us to take the initiative to offer preference, step out to lead with respect, go above and beyond to give honor. Let's follow his encouragement and go out of our way to show others their value in Christ.

Reflection:

How can I remember to view my brothers and sisters in Christ with high value as they have been bought with a great price?

In what way will I be intentional to treat others with the honor due the sacrifice of Jesus?

Prayer:

Lord, thank You for adopting me into Your family through the blood of Jesus. Help me to think thoughts that are honoring to You and to outdo myself in showing honor to my brothers and sisters. In Jesus' name, amen.

9. The Honorable Life

by Sandi Baete

"Who is wise and understanding among you? Let them show it by their good life, by deeds done in the humility that comes from wisdom." James 3:13 (NIV)

Honorable is a fancy word we don't hear, or use, often. And that makes sense because it is not a word we use to describe common things. In fact, I'm not sure I've ever used the word outside of reading my Bible. Maybe honorable isn't a word you use regularly either, so let's do a little exercise. What do you think of when you hear the word honorable? Here's some space to write what comes to mind:

_____

_____

_____

_____

In its simplest definition, honorable means deserving honor. I don't know about you, but I was taught to never define a word using the word I'm defining. While, technically, honor and honorable are different words, this definition doesn't tell us much. Honor describes honesty, fairness, and integrity in one's beliefs and actions. Basically, honor is when what we believe matches up with what we say and do in our everyday lives. Living with honor leads to being honorable. I want to live this way, but I often fall short.

Back to our exercise. What things did you describe as honorable? Maybe you thought of the way a judge is introduced, for example, the Honorable Judge Smith. You may have remembered someone who lives by an exceptionally high moral code, whose words and actions are always beyond criticism. A single circumstance may have come to mind, such as a student who admitted cheating when they weren't at risk of getting caught. While all these things are honorable, I'm pretty sure they aren't the honorable things Scripture is telling us to think about. Or maybe they are. But I'm getting ahead of myself.

If honor is having complete integrity in our beliefs and actions, there is only One who is entirely honorable. He always was, always is, and always will be Who He says He is. We may not know the will of God, but we can always trust He is good because He never changes. I don't think any of us would argue with the idea that we should think about God. He is the very definition of honorable. While I would love to sit and think about the Lord all day, that's not always very practical. And if you know anything about me at all, you know I love Jesus, I love books, and I love practicality. Not all in the same measure, of course.

So how can we practically think about what is honorable as we go about our daily lives? An even better question might be, how can we live with more honor in our daily lives? Our Scripture above, James 3:13, gives us some instruction. When we have wisdom about what honor really means, our good lives will show it. There won't be any "gray" areas, we won't follow the crowd just to fit in, and our actions and interactions will be marked by love and humility. It's not rocket science, but often easier said than done. Especially in the moment. When we don't want to be seen as being different, or intolerant, like we don't know how to take a joke or have fun. When we think no one is watching.

Take a moment to look back at the things you listed as being honorable. While we know Jesus is our ultimate example of all that is good, it's encouraging to see imperfect people living life well and having integrity in the hard things. What if we looked to their good works, not to put them on a pedestal, but to give us inspiration and courage to live with more honor? Because someone is always watching.

Reflection:

What is one area in my life that needs more integrity between my beliefs and actions?

What change(s) can I make to become more honorable in this area?

Prayer:

Lord, You are the only one Who is entirely honorable. Help me to honor You better by living what I believe. Help my words and actions be full of integrity so that any good seen in my life brings glory to You. In Jesus' name, amen.

10. Humming Birdbrain

by Sheri Trusty

"And to be renewed in the spirit of your minds, and to put on the new self, created after the likeness of God in true righteousness and holiness." Ephesians 4:23-24 (ESV)

I have a small bird oasis just off my back porch. On any given day, you may find me sitting outside watching Blue Jays swoop in for peanuts, Gray Catbirds stop by for slurps of grape jelly, and Red-bellied Woodpeckers cling to the suet feeders as they yank out bits of nut.

Flying above the activity is the Ruby-throated Hummingbird - a feisty, iridescent-winged bird that weighs less than a marshmallow and can dive through the air at a rate of 60 mph. Their short, stubby legs make it impossible for them to walk, but they can zoom from tree to flower to feeder in a few seconds' time. Occasionally, a couple of hummers will zip by within a couple inches of my head as they fight over the feeder that hangs on the side of my porch. I never worry they will run into me. Their flight precision is impeccable.

Far too often, my thoughts zoom from one thing to another as quickly as a hummingbird in flight, going from positive to foolish to ugly in a few seconds' time. Yet Philippians 4:8 says we are to actively, purposely think about things that are "right." "Right" – or "righteous" as it sometimes appears in Scripture – means "correct" in the original Greek. We are to intentionally generate correct, righteous thinking, but unlike hummingbirds in flight, my thoughts can have little precision. My thoughts can't focus on what is correct and right when they are freefalling.

Although many of us would be quick to admit the unfocused, constant scattering of our thoughts, I'm not sure we recognize how easily our thoughts can become ungodly.

In Ephesians 4:17, Paul warns us that we should no longer be like people who don't know God and live in the "futility of their minds." Those people, Paul says in the following verses, have darkened understanding, are alienated from the life of God, have hard hearts, and are callous and impure. That's a scary description, but the fact that Paul warns us to avoid this behavior proves that it is possible for us to become Christians who live like we have no clue about the goodness of Christ.

But Paul goes on to say it is also possible to *not* live this way. We can, he says, put off our "old self" and put on our "new self." We need to remember, he says, who we are now. We are children of God "created after the likeness of God in true righteousness and holiness." (Verses 22-24).

How do we do that? How do we put off our old, foolish ways and start living like a daughter of the mighty God? Paul says we do this by being renewed "in the spirit of your minds." Renewing our minds requires dependence on and collaboration with God. On one hand, we can't renew our own minds. We were born, full of foolishness, into a broken world. God has to change us, and in His tenderness, He chooses to change us through relationship. We spend time with Him, and in the midst of that love and grace, our darkened understanding is slowly transformed into the mind of Christ (I Corinthians 2:16).

Although God molds our new way of thinking, we still have to do our part to keep up with the changes, and that requires intentionality. We must actively, continually examine our thoughts and reroute them when necessary. We've got to catch our thoughts in the freefall, judge their darkness and direction, and put them back on the right path if need be. This is hard work, but it's vital work. We count pennies to control our budgets, and we count calories to govern our waistlines. We can count our thoughts to master our minds as well. Managing our thought life will take us another step closer to our "new self," where our thoughts are righteous and reflective of the One who made us new.

Reflection:

How has my thought life positively and negatively affected my behavior?

Prayer:

Lord, help me to take seriously the battle to control my mind, that I may be more for You and more like You. In Jesus' name, amen.

11. Right vs. Wrong

by Teresa Davis

"There is a path before each person that seems right, but it ends in death." Proverbs 14:12 (NLT)

Have you ever made a decision that you thought was the right one and come to realize it probably wasn't your best moment? Do you get paralyzed with the thought of making a wrong decision? In a world full of knowledge that is readily accessible by the click of a few keys on Google, we are overwhelmed with making the "wrong" choice. No one likes regret. I don't. But here's the truth: if we live our whole life never making a mistake, how will we learn to navigate life?

Many of our modern-day inventions came about by trial and error. In 1753, Benjamin Franklin discovered electricity with his famous kite-flying experiments; however, it was many years later, many trials that failed before a usable form of electricity was eventually invented. First in the form of a battery in 1800, followed by Thomas Edison's light bulb in 1879.

If our children never made a wrong decision, we wouldn't have teachable moments where we express our love for them yet allow them to feel the consequences of their choices. When Paul was writing to the people of Philippi, he was teaching them how to have godly habits that would produce peace and contentment. One of the habits includes thinking about things that are right and noble. This concept brings to the surface the conflict in our society today. Is there right and wrong in a moral sense?

At the beginning of this devotion, I was mentioning choices of everyday life that we can learn from, but Paul was encouraging us to focus on a different kind of right. The amplified version says it like this: "whatever is right and confirmed by God's Word." Philippians 4:8. Our society would like to take us down a path where there is no right or wrong, but we know, according to God's Word, that this is not true.

In order to support the belief that there is right and wrong, we must believe in a God who established justice from day one. He created the standard by making rules in the garden and by writing the 10 commandments. He knew we were going to need some boundaries in order to live our lives in a healthy way. He's a good and gracious God, and, because He is our Creator, He knows our needs. Left to our own ability to make decisions, without our Creator involved, our choices may lead down a path that seems right but will end in disaster.

Now let me be clear, God loves a repentant heart. "Fools make fun of guilt, but the godly acknowledge it and seek reconciliation." Proverbs 14:9 (NLT)

Our heavenly Father is our example of how to love in spite of our sinful nature. He waits for our repentance so we may be reconciled back to Him. However, there is a way that seems right to man. If we solely rely on our own strength and wisdom we will be misguided. Paul was giving us the guidelines to follow to have a peaceful, abundant life. Our thinking can ruin a peaceful, abundant life. How do we focus on whatever is right? By consuming God's Word, centering our minds on it, and implanting His words in our hearts.

Reflection:

How will I focus on whatever is right, confirmed by God's Word today?

Prayer:

Lord Jesus, open the eyes of my heart as I seek You today. May I find peace and contentment by consuming Your good and perfect gifts. In Jesus' name, amen.

12. What is Right

by Katie Mason

"A person may think their own ways are right, but the Lord weighs the heart." Proverbs 21:2 (NIV)

Have you ever heard the phrase, "you do you and I'll do me"? Or maybe you have seen a meme with the phrase "this is my truth"? Both of these are very dangerous statements to make as believers in Christ. As Christians, we cannot be swayed by the world's understanding of truth. We must stand on what is right. We must be firmly planted on the Rock of our Truth, Jesus Christ.

When we as humans start following what we believe to be right, our course quickly takes a detour towards what feels right instead of what is right. When we allow our minds to be the guide to how we should believe, it doesn't take long for us to go down the roads of what experiences will bring us pleasure. When we are led by what our neighbors think is right, we can often start claiming allegiance to things that might seem true but are actually a half-lie. Our hearts are deceptive. Jeremiah 17:9 says "The heart is deceitful above all things and beyond cure. Who can understand it?" We cannot depend on our hearts to guide us or tell us what is right.

As disciples in Christ, we are to walk a very narrow road. It is lined with pits of deception, temptation, and opportunity for moral ambiguity. It is a road that might be difficult to walk, but we do not walk it in our own power. That is why we must know what is right. Why we, like the psalmist, must ask the Holy Spirit to "Test me, Lord, and try me, examine my heart and mind." (Psalm 26:2) Without the intervention of the Holy Spirit in our hearts and minds, we will become like the church in Laodicea which was told it would be spit out of God's mouth because it was lukewarm (Revelation 3:16). Nobody wants to drink a lukewarm cup of coffee, especially not the Author of all good and right things.

When we are self-guided on what is right, we are being deceived by our hearts. Because we are fallen people, every effort in our own power to do what is right will end up failing. It might seem right for a while. It might even bring blessings to our lives. But if our right actions are not based in the Truth of God, we are simply deceiving ourselves.

Let us be followers of the only One who is right. We have the perfect example of Jesus who is the only One to have walked this earth completely dependent on the guidance of the Holy Spirit. Jesus, the One who fulfilled all of the Law and the prophets, teaching us the right way to live with the Father. It's my hope and prayer that we will not be like the Pharisees that thought they were fulfilling the Law. Our God's yoke is not about a list of rules to do what is right. His yoke is easy and light. Just as Jesus is the One who got things right by loving others, by caring for the widow and orphan, and by spending time with the Father minute by minute, so may we walk in that same narrow path that He did.

My sisters, we can choose what is right because we serve the most righteous God. When we embrace the truth of Scripture, we begin to see how we might live rightly. We don't do this for any kind of earthly praise or recognition. We do this so when we do go to Heaven, once again living in true harmony with our Creator, we can hear the Father say, "Well done, my good and faithful servant." (Matthew 25:23a)

Reflection:

Where do I need to surrender to God what I think is right? I ask the Holy Spirit to search my heart and mind for any places that need to be made right in Truth.

Prayer:

Dear God, search my heart. Reveal to me any dark places that need Your light. Please show me what is right versus what I believe to be right. Lord, You walked on earth living in the right relationship with the Father. Thank You for the Holy Spirit who is guiding me to do the same. In Jesus' name, amen.

13. Waiting on the Lord

by Stephanie Heitz

"Create in me a pure heart, O Lord, and renew a steadfast spirit within me." Psalm 51:10 (NIV)

Many of us dream of motherhood from the time we're young. We begin a sweet narrative in our minds, painting a neat, little picture of what things might look like when we grow up. The perfect marriage, an immaculate home with magazine-worthy decor, and two, three, or maybe even four respectfully obedient kids, who love Jesus with all their hearts, and grow up to be missionaries, Sunday School teachers, or maybe even pastors.

We learn pretty quickly that being a mother isn't for the faint of heart. I don't know a single job on the planet that requires such long hours with no salary, hardly any sleep, and little to no appreciation from the precious darlings we spend our lives tirelessly pouring into! We experience the purest kind of unconditional love this side of Heaven as we fall deeply in love with each of our babies. Because of this profound love, we ultimately put ourselves at great risk of heartbreak when things don't go as planned.

Imagine my broken heart when my 15-yr-old daughter came to me and declared, "I don't believe the same way you do." She might as well have ripped my heart right out of my chest and stomped on it! My life's work had just crumbled to the ground with this simple, yet impactful, statement. Or how about the heaviness I began to feel as I observed my 21-yr-old son sleeping-in week after week on Sunday morning, instead of feeding his spirit at church? When I approached him and asked, "What's going on with you and Jesus?" He replied, "Not much. I'm not really sure I've ever felt His presence in my life." Now, I've always taught my kids to be honest, but this was quite agonizing to hear. Another dagger through my heart.

The Holy Spirit is so faithful in the wise counsel He provides day in and day out. He's quick to remind me to cling to the promises of God, pray without ceasing, and love my children fiercely right where they are. They know very well what I stand for and now is not the time to cram it down their throats. I simply need to let them know they are seen, heard, and tremendously valued.

Every single one of us must have our own journey with Jesus. Adversity may cause us to hold tightly to our faith, allowing it to be our compass, or flee from it quickly, overcome by the mindset that God has abandoned us in our suffering.

God doesn't have any grandchildren. We cannot ride on the coattails of our parents' faith and expect to secure a reservation in Heaven if we haven't made our own personal decision to become a child of God.

Oh, precious mothers! Don't grow weary as you wait on the Lord to awaken the faith of one or more of your kids. Together, let us ask the Lord to create in us pure hearts that hope, pure hearts that trust, and pure hearts that don't grow dismayed or discouraged when things don't go as we had envisioned.

May the Lord renew in each of us a steadfast spirit to stand firmly on His promises and abide in His perfect plan.

Reflection:

Have I given up hope or lost confidence that the Lord keeps His promises and is continually working things together for good in my life and the lives of my children?

Prayer:

Dear Heavenly Father, hear my cry for help! Draw my children unto You that they may experience the greatest love of all. Increase their desire to walk in a right relationship with You and fill them with a peace that passes understanding. In Jesus' name, amen.

14. Indicator Lights

by Sheri Trusty

"The commandment of the Lord is **pure**, enlightening the eyes." Psalm 19:8b (NASB)

At first glance, Philippians 4:8 appears as simply a beautiful, uplifting passage. It shows us that God wants our minds filled with light and love and godliness. But when I step beyond simply reading the verse into an effort to apply it, I recognize how difficult the task is. I know how easily my thoughts slip into ugly patterns of selfishness, complaint, or judgment. My mind doesn't naturally embrace the godly call of Philippians 4:8, and I find that the passage is beautiful but also challenging.

Where do we find the standard for this high calling of godly thought? Where do we find encouragement to mold our minds with such high ideals? We find it right where we would expect: in Scripture.

"The Law of the Lord is perfect, restoring the soul; the testimony of the Lord is sure, making wise the simple. The precepts of the Lord are right, rejoicing the heart; the commandment of the Lord is pure, enlightening the eyes. The fear of the Lord is clean, enduring forever; the judgments of the Lord are true; they are righteous altogether." Psalm 19:7-9

There is an extraordinary similarity between Philippians 4:8 and Psalm 19:7-9. The Philippians verse tells us how to think, and the Psalm passage describes Scripture, yet they are complimentary passages with three exact words: true, right, and pure.

God sets high standards for us, but He doesn't make demands and send us on our way floundering in the fog of our own ungodliness. The Bible says He walks before us (Deuteronomy 31:8), stays near us (Psalm 145:18), helps us (Psalm 54:4), and teaches us (Psalm 32:8). To help us nurture a godly mindset, which will, in turn, cultivate a godly life, God has given us indicators that convey the direction of our thoughts. Besides teaching us through Scripture and the Holy Spirit, He has also given us the indicators of our actions, our mouths, and our emotions. Each of those things indicates where our thoughts are focused. How often have you said, "How could I have done that?", "I can't believe I said that!", or "I am overwhelmed with emotion right now!"

It is easy in these failure moments to turn to discouragement or shame, but that's not what God wants for us. He longs to grow life and joy in us, so He wants us to use the indicators of actions, words, and emotions as tools to see where we need to readjust our thinking so that we're thinking more about Him. Just like the little indicator light on our cars tell us that it's time to change the oil, our out-of-control actions, words, and emotions can tell us it's time to change our thoughts.

When we do, say, and feel things that we know are not honoring to God, we need to step back, examine what just happened, and look for root causes – or maybe the root rot. As we look at what occurred, we need to ask ourselves, "Why?" Am I believing a lie that doesn't align with Scripture? Am I not trusting God to handle this? Am

I mad that God won't give me what I want? Am I being motivated by pride?

There are many unhealthy and ungodly reasons why we act, talk, and feel foolishly, but God wants us to use those failures as self-teaching moments that will lead us to grow in purity. Psalm 19:8 tells us that Scripture "is pure, enlightening the eyes." In other words, Scripture teaches us. As we respond to our ungodly behavior with the purity of God's Word, it helps us become pure.

When those "How could I?" moments hit, don't turn to discouragement and shame. Be sorry for them. Fix the mess if you've made one. But remember that those actions, words, and emotions are spiritual little indicator lights that God turned on to convey this simple message to you, "Change your thoughts and think about Me."

Reflection:

Which of my actions, words, and emotions caused my indicator light to kick on today?

Prayer:

Lord, teach me to recognize that my foolish actions, words, and emotions can be used as tools to turn my thoughts to You. In Jesus' name, amen.

15. What is a Pure Heart?

by Katie Mason

"Flee the evil desires of youth and pursue righteousness, faith, love, and peace, along with those who call on the Lord out of a pure heart." 2 Timothy 2:22 (NIV)

When I was a young Christian, I was surrounded with the idea of purity. I needed to have pure thoughts, pure actions, and motives. I needed to be pure, remain pure, and pursue purity. It was a system of rules and regulations that encouraged me to be in the world but not of it. There was a checklist of behaviors and thoughts that needed to be ticked off each day to ensure that I would have a pure heart. There was even a prayer for me to pray that asked God to forgive whatever action I had done that I didn't realize was a sin of impurity. It was all very thorough and exhausting. Living by a set of black-and-white rules didn't prepare me for all the gray areas of life. It also filled me with a self-righteousness that would give a Pharisee a run for his money.

While the pursuit of purity is a noble and commanded goal set out for believers, I think sometimes we take the idea of purity and make it about how well we can follow the rules instead of its intended purpose which is to bring us closer to God. The rules give us standards by which we can judge and be judged by other believers. When this happens, our hearts may be pure from the sins of lust, greed, gluttony, and sloth. But there are often the sins of envy, jealousy, comparison, and self-righteousness to contend with. Even in the solo pursuits of our lives, we can still fall prey to temptation and keep it secret from others. In all of this, the pursuit of purity becomes the god in our lives rather than the God we are trying to grow closer to.

When we make purity the idol instead of a pursuit of being Christ-like, we miss out on the beauty of living with grace. When we are too busy judging other believers because they don't match up to our standards of purity, then we miss out on the gift of forgiveness and mercy we have received. When we make purity about rules, we are then set up as the ones who can save ourselves.

We should absolutely pursue the attributes of a mature Christian, but we should do so humbly. With the attitude of one who, like Paul says in Philippians 2:5-6 "In your relationships with one another, have the same mindset as Christ Jesus: Who, being in very nature God, did not consider equality with God something to be used to his own advantage." If Jesus Christ Himself did not wave His flag of divinity around to compare others to Himself, how, then, can we?

I ask again, what is a pure heart? It is found in surrender. Surrender to God and His ways. In each of Paul's epistles to the young Church, we find specific instructions on how to live a purely surrendered life. We learn that we should lead quiet lives. Take care of our families and those that need help. We are to care for widows and orphans. We are to walk humbly, act justly, and seek mercy as it says in Micah 6:8.

Purity is not about checking off boxes on a list. It's about developing a lifestyle that is completely surrendered to the mandates of Scripture. Surrendering to the Lordship of the only One who has walked this earth completely pure. When that is our goal, our lives remain focused on God which allows us to see how impure we each are. That gives us a swift opportunity to repent and continue on in His ways. Then, we can begin humbly walking under our God's banner of grace, mercy, and forgiveness.

Reflection:

Where do I need to be purified? What needs to be brought out so I can walk with God and have a pure heart?

Prayer:

Lord Jesus, I repent. I lay down at the foot of the cross each behavior, thought pattern, habit, and secret longing. Take what is impure and remove it from me, Lord. Search me and know me so that I might remain close to You, Father. I want to remain in right standing with You. In Jesus' name, amen.

16. Who God Says You Are

by Cassia Elder

"You are altogether beautiful, my darling; there is no flaw in you." Song of Songs 4:7 (NIV)

Song of Songs (also referred to as Song of Solomon) is the one book in Scripture that is sure to make most of us blush. This poetic passage is a passionate love song about a Bride and her Groom, the King. The captivating celebration of married life is filled with vivid imagery as King Solomon describes his consuming love for his favorite wife.

But there is more than one love story depicted in Song of Solomon. This book of the Bible is categorized as poetry, but it is also prophetic of Jesus' relationship with His Church. Collectively, followers of Jesus are the Bride of Christ; He is the King of kings. As part of His Church, the Bride and Body of Christ, God sees us in a very holy but equally intimate way, with the beauty described in Solomon's Song. You are altogether lovely (CEV), flawless in His eyes!

This truth is confirmed for us in Ephesians 1:4-5. "For he chose us in him before the creation of the world to be holy and blameless in his sight. In love he predestined us for adoption to sonship through Jesus Christ, in accordance with his pleasure and will." (NIV)

It may be difficult to think of ourselves the way God sees us. After all, we've met us. We are all too familiar with our own sins and shortcomings. Honestly, I have often called myself by my mistakes; maybe you have, too. When I knocked over a glass and shards went skating across the kitchen counter, "I'm so clumsy." When I threw the brownie box into the trash before reading the directions and had to dig it back out to see how much oil to add, "Stupid girl."

But God doesn't view us according to our failures. He sees us through Jesus' sacrifice on the cross that pays the penalty of our sins and washes us clean.

Read these declarations of who God says we are:

Fearfully and wonderfully made. (Psalm 139:14)

A friend of Jesus. (John 15:15)

Justified and redeemed. (Romans 3:24)

Accepted. (Romans 15:7)

A new creation. (2 Corinthians 5:17)

Righteous. (2 Corinthians 5:21)

His masterpiece. (Ephesians 2:10 NLT)

Chosen, holy, and dearly loved. (Colossians 3:12)

A child of God. (1 John 3:1)

It's not enough to know these things, we have to believe them. Did you know that you believe what you say more than what you hear from anyone else? You don't think you're a liar, so if it comes out of your mouth, your mind believes it's true.

Link arms with me as we replace the negative things we've thought and said about ourselves with the truth of God's Word. Let's choose a declaration of who we are in Christ and repeat it over ourselves, out loud when we can, until our thoughts are changed and we believe it.

The Bible is full of truths about who we are in Christ. Search the Scriptures and find a few verses that resonate with you.

Sweet Sister, you are who God says you are!

Reflection:

In what ways do I struggle to think of myself the way God sees me?

What Bible truth will I choose as a declaration to repeat over myself until my thoughts are changed and I believe it?

Prayer:

Holy God, thank You for the blood of Jesus that is the lens through which You see me. Help me to believe that I am who You say I am and to think of myself according to Your truth. In Jesus' name, amen.

17. Beyond Beautiful

by Sandi Baete

"There is a way that appears to be right, but in the end it leads to death." Proverbs 14:12 (NIV)

My husband and I moved into our current home in the summer of 2014. The home was about 10 years old and in good shape, so we basically just moved in and lived our life for a few years. In 2019, we decided that it was time for a few updates and improvements: new flooring, a new countertop, and a fresh coat of paint in a couple of rooms. At this point, you can probably tell I definitely do not have the gift of the prophecy. Otherwise, I would have known that in 2020 we were going to have all kinds of time to work on home improvement. Which would have been a better option than all the binge-watching and snacking we did.

In the three years since our home improvement projects, I have been very satisfied with our home. It isn't beautiful like the homes you see on HGTV, but it reflects who we are and what's important to us. Recently though, I decided to make a little list of a few new projects I had been thinking about. They included such important things as raising our curtain rods higher and buying longer curtains, upholstering footstools to match a particular chair in our living room, and redesigning a closet to better utilize the space. A few minutes later, I quickly crossed off the entire list.

It wasn't that I didn't want to do those things; I simply realized I didn't want to for a good reason. I wanted to "upgrade" because I was looking at my home from a worldly perspective. A perspective that says everything in our lives should be beautiful. A perspective that says if we haven't updated something recently, we need to find something to update. I was perfectly happy with my home until I watched a home makeover show and scanned Pinterest.

As people, we long for beauty and perfection but are never satisfied. We seek beautiful living spaces, gourmet meals, 5-star vacation resorts, and picture-perfect everything while our souls long for that which is lovely. Lovely goes beyond what we can see, further than physical attributes. Lovely is less tangible but no less real. It may appeal to our eyes, but even more to our hearts and minds.

Let's play a little game. In each pair of words/phrases below, circle the one that best defines the concept of "lovely":

Gourmet meal eaten alone
-or-
A simple meal with friends

Spending $50 on a new sweater
-or-
Donating $50 to a homeless shelter

Perceived Perfection
-or-
Authenticity

You get the idea. Thinking about and seeking what is lovely nourishes us, it feeds our soul. It's not always free, but it's always worth it. We are known and loved; we help care for others. Beauty may give us something, but it almost always asks too high a price. We are alone, broke, exhausted, and never feel loved for who we are. I'm not telling you not to appreciate your newest home improvement project, your fresh from the salon hair, or even the cute trendy outfit you got on sale. We live in the world and are going to want some of its stuff. But maybe, just maybe, instead of pursuing the things that are beautiful, we try God's way. Let's begin to attend more to our souls than our senses. I have no doubt we'll find thinking of what is lovely to be a beautiful way to live.

Reflection:

Where are you seeking beauty in your life?

How can you begin to look for and cultivate the lovely instead?

Prayer:

Lord, I want to be lovely on Your terms. Help me to be more concerned with being gracious and peaceful and gentle and restful and fully engaged with the people You put in my life than I am about pretty things, a beautiful home, trendy clothes, or anything else the world deems necessary for a lovely life. In Jesus' name, amen.

18. Vengeance is Mine

by Teresa Davis

"Righteousness and justice are the foundation of your throne. Unfailing love and truth walk before you as attendants." Psalm 89:14 (NLT)

In Paul's letter to the church of Philippi, in chapter 4 verse 8, we are given a list of eight things we are to fix our thoughts upon. Take note that the verse before addresses anxiety. Paul understood the human condition and wrote first about our anxious thoughts followed by what we need to think about. This requires the ability to recognize the thoughts that are producing anxiety and choose to focus on what calms us and brings relief. Whatever is lovely is included in the list and this is where I want to focus our thoughts today.

The title of today's devotion may not seem to fit but stay with me. Often our thoughts are fixed on what troubles us the most. The weight of carrying an offense that has never been made right can consume us. We play out scenarios in our minds to make it right. When justice is not served, it can leave us feeling hopeless and defeated with a mindset that it will never be rectified.

What if you believed that it wasn't your responsibility to make it right? What if you believed that justice will be served in a manner that you cannot comprehend? What if you believed that the foundation of God's throne is righteousness and justice? What if you believed that the truth will be made known for all to see in a way only God can do?

The offense to one of His own does not go unnoticed.

"Beloved, never avenge yourselves, but leave it to the wrath of God, for it is written, "Vengeance is mine, I will repay, says the Lord." Romans 12:19 (ESV)

"The Lord is a jealous and avenging God; the Lord is avenging and wrathful; the Lord takes vengeance on his adversaries and keeps wrath for his enemies." Nahum 1:2 (ESV)

The righteous right hand of God signifies power. It's the hand that brings justice. It's the hand that holds us up out of the deep waters. It's the mighty hand from which nothing can be removed, and it's the hand that will one day reach down and take us home. Never underestimate the power of our God. It is far beyond anything we can imagine.

I challenge you today, when the overwhelming thoughts of offense come to rob you of your peace, to choose again. Choose to think on whatsoever is lovely. Fix your thoughts on what inspires you, on what gives you peace. Leave the weight of righting the wrongs behind. Our Father will bring justice in a way we are not capable of. Choose to think of His righteous right hand and His great love for you. When you fill up on these thoughts, it will clear your heart and mind to bring more of His restful goodness into your life.

Reflection:

I will consider the option today to "choose again" and decide how I will practice it.

I will choose thoughts that are lovely to me, that bring me peace, and commit to focusing on them.

Prayer:

Father, make me aware today of when I need to "choose again." Help me, Jesus, to rest in knowing that You will make the wrongs right in a way I never could. In Jesus' name, amen.

19. Trusting God with My Trouble

by Angie Baughman

"Cast all your anxiety on Him, because He cares about you." 1 Peter 5:7 (NASB)

Have you heard the sentiment that trust is built in drops and lost in buckets?

I have often thought about the spiritual truth in that statement. God drips proof of His faithfulness into my life continually. I see Him in my children's eyes, feel Him in a gentle breeze, and hear Him in praise music coming through my earbuds. Drip. Drip. Drip.

Because there have been times when I trusted someone and ended up with that bucket of trust dumped out on my head, I have considered the wisdom in believing in others and God. I feared facing disappointment again because experiences like that make us cautious.

But if we're willing to hold up God's promises to the events in our lives, we will see that His Word never fails us. He is always who He says He is, and always doing what He says He will do. His reputation is commendable. Drip. Drip. Drip.

I love the reminder in 1 Peter 5:7 that tells us to cast our anxiety on God. The Greek word for cast comes from a word that means "to fling with a deliberate hurl." Think of it like stumbling upon an explosive device, picking it up, and with all your might, throwing it as far away from you as you possibly can.

Anxiety is an obstacle to connecting with the faithful trustworthiness of God's commendable reputation. When we hold on to anxiety, we stop accumulating His drops of faithfulness - not because He stops offering them, but because we stop receiving them. We become focused on ourselves and our concerns and forget to depend on the One who has proven Himself trustworthy.

If it isn't easy for you to trust in God's faithfulness, here are a few places in Scripture that help me remember God shows up and does the miraculous in situations that undoubtedly created a great deal of anxiety:

- In Exodus 14, God's people cross a sea on dry land.
- In 1 Kings 18, God's fire consumes Elijah's offering while everyone is watching.
- In Mark 5, Jesus heals a woman who was bleeding for twelve years.
- In John 20, many disciples began to encounter the Risen Lord.

God has proven Himself able to assist us in our trouble, but He lets us decide if we will put our trust in and cast our anxiety on His excellent reputation.

Reflection:

When I am anxious and scared, I can remember God's reputation of being faithful and know He is the same God yesterday, today, and always. (Hebrews 13:8)

Prayer:

Faithful God, You never let me down. Forgive me for holding onto my anxiety instead of trusting in Your promises. Thank You for being good, gracious, and loving. Help me remember to take my worries and concerns to You. In Jesus' name, amen.

20. The Good Reports

by Sheri Trusty

"Do we begin again to commend ourselves?" 2 Corinthians 3:1a (KJV)

I often hear the same response when I ask people if I can write a story about them for our local newspaper. "I don't want people to think I'm bragging," they say. That's a lovely, albeit unnecessary, response. I explain that the story will encourage and uplift the readers without a hint of self-promotion, but, like Paul in the verse above, they don't want to commend themselves.

Philippians 4:8 tells us we are to think about things that are commendable (NASB). I especially like the KJV translation of this verse, which says we are to think of things that are "of good report." I've worked as a newspaper correspondent for several years, reporting on local people who are doing incredible things in their communities. I always say I write the good news, but I could just as easily say I write "the good reports."

It's an exceptionally fun job. My work gives me the opportunity to meet the best people across a two-county region. I get to sit down with them, hear about their lives, and then share their stories in the newspaper. Basically, I get to commend them to the world.

Spending hours upon hours talking with good people and writing their stories gives me ample opportunity to think about commendable things. My brain is beautifully bombarded with good news, and within that deluge of commendable images, I've recognized a common thread among the best people I've met: they are marked by humility.

In 2 Corinthians 3:1, Paul did not want to commend himself. On the contrary, he said in verses 2 and 3 that he didn't need a formal letter of commendation to prove the worth of his ministry because the people he ministered to were living, tangible, commendable proof of his efforts. His commendation, Paul said, came not in "tables of stone, but in fleshy tables of the heart." (vs. 3)

Those are the kinds of people I interview every week, people whose hearts and actions commend their lives. They tell me their stories with modesty and meekness, and I find it easy to commend with my pen what is seen with my eyes.

And I recognize, over and over again, that humility is the indispensable cornerstone of a great life.

"He has told you, O man, what is good; and what does the Lord require of you but to do justice, and to love kindness, and to walk humbly with your God?" Micah 6:8 (ESV)

I could draw from my years of newspaper work and give countless examples of people who "walk humbly with your God," but some of the best illustrations of meekness come from people in addiction recovery. Many times, I have walked away from an interview overwhelmed by the person's willingness to be real and raw about their addiction. They let me put their photo, their mistakes, and their regrets on the front page because they know that someone who is still stuck in addiction may see it and find hope for recovery in the God of hope. These people humble themselves, choose grace over honor, and throw out the lifeline that once saved their own souls.

That is love. That is Christlike. That is commendable beyond words.

Humility breeds a commendable life. Until we finally recognize our utter helplessness and lack of worth outside of God and begin to think about and embrace His limitless mercy and love, we won't reach a real depth of impact on those around us. Until we stop trying to commend ourselves and, instead, live in a way where our hearts and actions commend us, we'll only show the world a distorted image of God's love.

Reflection:

Where have I seen the power of humility exemplified in someone's life?

How can my thoughts of that life influence my own behavior?

Prayer:

Lord, help me to see the potential of humility to create a commendable life marked by a love for You and a love for others. In Jesus' name, amen.

21. Think Commendable

by Cassia Elder

"Do not let any unwholesome talk come out of your mouths, but only what is helpful for building others up according to their needs, that it may benefit those who listen." Ephesians 4:29 (NIV)

When I was a little girl in church, I always remember hearing the first half of this verse used (out of context) to remind us not to say bad words. The second half was never attached.

Every other place in the Bible where we find this word for "unwholesome," it is translated as "bad," literally referring to rotten fruit. And the word translated "helpful" means intrinsically good. When we look at those two ideas together, we see that our focus should never solely be on what not to do, but on what we should do instead.

Here (in full context), Paul was talking specifically about the way we treat people and how our words can impact others. What we choose to speak can tear them down or build them up. Our speech can be of benefit or harm to our listeners. We are urged to eliminate worthless, rotten talk and to limit our conversation to what is building up and beneficial.

But what does this have to do with our focus to "think about these things?"

Well, the thing is, the way we talk to and about other people comes from the overflow of what we think about them.

Jesus said in Matthew 12:34, "The mouth speaks what the heart is full of." The words of our mouths directly reflect the meditations of our hearts.

Look, sometimes relationships are difficult. When others irritate, offend, or hurt us, we can allow negative thoughts to consume our minds. Those thoughts then flow from our mouths in negativity toward that person. So, Paul tells us in the Ephesians verse above that what we say should be good and helpful. And where our key verse for the devotional, Philippians 4:8, tells us to think about what is "commendable," other translations use the words "admirable" or "of good report."

The truth is simple. If we want to speak good words to others, we need to think good thoughts about them.

I have seen this principle at play in my own life.

When my thoughts about others are centered on the condemnable—focusing on their faults and failures—I am quick to criticize and to be short with my replies. But, when I concentrate on the commendable in others—considering what I admire and appreciate—I am more apt to praise and to give a kind response.

Switching our thoughts from negative to positive takes practice. When I struggle to choose commendable thoughts about others over the condemnable thoughts that run rampant in my mind, I need to flip the script.

One practical exercise I have learned is to pause and intentionally choose to think three positive things about the other person. Writing or journaling helps me to slow my mind, engage additional senses, and solidify truth. So, when I get the chance, I add these three things to my gratitude list.

Let's look for the best in others. Choose to think good thoughts about and to speak good words to the people in our lives.

Reflection:

How will I intentionally choose commendable thoughts about others that will result in speaking what is helpful?

Prayer:

Lord, I want to speak to others only what is building up and beneficial. I know that begins with how I think. Please help me to choose thoughts that are honoring to You and to think the best of others. Remind me to see the commendable in those I encounter. In Jesus' name, amen.

22. Holy Shoddy is Still Shoddy

by Katie Mason

"Now eagerly desire the greater gifts. And yet I will show you the most excellent way.'" I Corinthians 12:31 (NIV)

When I was in college, I was part of a choir. This was a requirement for my super practical pursuit of getting a church music degree. The choir I was a part of had over a hundred members, yet, the director could pick out if someone was singing a wrong note or had the rhythm incorrect. He had the ears of a wolf and the focus of a cheetah pursuing its prey. It was both frightening and exhilarating to be under that level of scrutiny and training.

One time in particular, the choir was not getting the song we were meant to be rehearsing. The director took his baton and slammed it on the music stand, shouting, "Holy shoddy is still shoddy!" The room became utterly silent. As the director regained his lost composure, I committed that phrase to memory. In both my heart and mind, I fixed that phrase as a mantra over my life. Because I so desperately wanted the approval of authority in my life, I became solely focused on pursuing perfection. I was determined to live my life as an example of excellence. That meant my wardrobe, family, grades, work, and even church activity would be excellent. And it would be excellent, no matter the cost to create that ideal.

When we think about what is holy, perfect, or excellent, we often think of God or Jesus as the perfect sacrifice for our sins. Sometimes that leads to us wanting to achieve holiness on this side of Heaven. We strive to attain the rewards of Heaven while still living in the brokenness of Earth. All of this self-focus on attaining what cannot be found on this side of God's Kingdom can leave us anxious, depressed, angry, or disillusioned. The root of our discontent is that we try to dig our own wells of living water with broken tools. We are not alone in this struggle. Our generation is not the first to deal with this broken system. In Jeremiah 2:13 (NLT) it says, "For my people have done two evil things: They have abandoned me-the fountain of living water. And they have dug for themselves cracked cisterns that can hold no water at all!"

When we strive to create holiness in our own power, it will always end up shoddy. You and I do not have the ability to live the most excellent way without the Holy Spirit to teach us how to stay on the path of excellence.

The love, grace, and mercy of our Father is waiting there for us. The only way we can begin to understand the most excellent way is by learning from our Father what His excellent way is. It is a way of gentleness, with both others and ourselves. It is a way of mercy that gives us the eyes to see ourselves and others as God sees us.

The most excellent way cannot be found in our own power. It can only be revealed to us when we are given spiritual eyes to see. While we are on a journey towards becoming like God, that journey is not meant to be a burden we carry alone. It is the light burden of Jesus. The one who told us that His burden is easy and His yoke is light (Matthew 11:30) because Jesus walks with us on the path towards holiness. The most excellent way is a way of leaning into the cross and recognizing how much we need the help of the Holy Spirit to guide us until we return home to Heaven.

Reflection:

What ideals or self-focused behaviors do I need to relinquish?

Prayer:

Father God, please forgive me when my pursuit of Your excellence becomes the pursuit of perfect. Show me where I need to lay down the ideals of my culture for the truth of Your way. Jesus, teach me how to love, to show mercy, and to have grace for others the way You have each of these things for me. Holy Spirit, remind me to stay humble. To stay in my lane and not look at anyone or thing on this earth that might distract me in my pursuit of You. In Jesus' name, amen.

23. Simply Excellent

by Sandi Baete

"Whatever you do, work at it with all your heart, as working for the Lord, not for human masters." Colossians 3:23 (NIV)

My husband recently had an item to return to a large home improvement store. He approached the customer service counter, and, when the young man working there looked at him but did not acknowledge him or offer any verbal greeting, my husband proceeded to explain he had a return. The employee processed the return, handed my husband a receipt, and completed the transaction without ever uttering a single word. Now, I don't know if the young man was simply having a bad day, or was poorly trained by the company he worked for. It's even possible the position of customer service representative required a skill set or personality traits he lacked. Regardless of the reason, and despite the fact the young man technically performed his job and refunded my husband's money, I think we can agree he did not perform it in an excellent manner.

How does this apply to us? How do we approach our daily activities? Do we look to complete each job and conversation quickly and with the least amount of thought and effort? Or do we approach each task and interaction with intention and care? What does it really mean to live in an excellent way and how can we make that a reality in our daily lives? Unlike many theological questions, this one is answered quickly and plainly by Scripture.

The greatest hindrance to living, serving, and loving others in an excellent way is our attitude. Our attitude determines our approach. It doesn't matter if we are doing laundry, helping our child with homework, or serving customers at our job. Colossians 3:23 tells us to approach all we do with the attitude that we are doing it for the Lord, to work at each endeavor with all our heart. When we live this way, everything we do will be done in an excellent manner. Let's consider some practical ways this might play out in our lives.

Doing laundry is a good place to start. I've heard some people love doing laundry, but I've never met those people, so I think it's reasonable to assume most of us don't approach this task with the best attitude. Definitely not with the thought of working at it with all our heart or that we're doing it for Jesus. But that's exactly what Colossians 3:23 says. So, we're doing laundry for Jesus. How does that differ from the way you do laundry for your family currently? Maybe it means being more diligent with stain removal, or folding clothes more neatly, or doing laundry more regularly. It could be as simple, and powerful, as praying for each person in your home as you fold the towels they will use.

We all have those people in our life we tend to give less than our best attention to. A talkative neighbor who goes on and on about topics of little significance, or a child needing help with homework. We act interested, but are distracted by our thoughts, the show we're streaming, or our phones. If Jesus were asking for homework help, I'm pretty sure we would give him our full attention, carefully explaining how to do the work, and making sure He comprehended before we moved on with our lives.

What about our jobs? We've already imagined doing Jesus' laundry and helping Him with homework, so let's go back to where we started our devotional today, with the story of the young customer service rep who served my husband recently. A smile and a simple greeting, followed by a speedy transaction and a sincere "Thank you" would have easily and quickly elevated his actions from indifferent to excellent. As Christians, we can give grace and even imagine reasons for his sub-par job performance, which helps us excuse his poor service. But as a follower of Jesus, excuses and inferior performance should not be terms associated with our employment, or any other area of our life.

Excellent. As if for the Lord, with all your heart. Whatever you do.

Reflection:

What are some ways I can begin to approach everyday tasks with all my heart?

Prayer:

Lord, I want to serve You and those around me in an excellent way. Even in the mundane and ordinary things of everyday life, may I complete each task as though it is for You, because everything is for You. In Jesus' name, amen.

24. One Single Mind

by Sheri Trusty

"Yea doubtless, and I count all things but loss for the excellency of the knowledge of Christ Jesus my Lord: for whom I have suffered the loss of all things, and do count them but dung, that I may win Christ." Philippians 3:8 (KJV)

I recently met an automotive engineer named Dan who willingly chose to stop pursuing promotions so he could have more time with his family. He was a successful and well-respected professional who could have gained an even more lucrative and prestigious career, but he set aside his aspirations to focus on his wife and children.

Within a year, he had spiraled into depression.

Suffering the loss of future success and all that could come with it brought him to, what he described as, a dark place. Yet, at the bottom of that darkness, he discovered a profound awareness of God's love. He said he had previously been an intellectual believer in God, but now he had a genuine, life-altering knowledge of Christ. What he gained in Christ was immeasurably beyond what he lost in his career.

The word "loss" is used in two flip-flop phrases in Philippians 3:8. In the first instance, "all things but loss," the word refers to damage. The "all things" that Paul talks about in this verse are the things we want and pursue, the things we put before our relationship with Jesus. These things damage us.

Later in the verse, Paul talks about the "loss of all things." Here, loss means to cast something away or give up our right to it. It is a willing release of something we want. Taken together, the verse tells us to recognize the damaging potential of the things we crave more than a knowledge of Christ, and the verse encourages us to release those things so we can "win Christ."

Philippians 4:8 says we are to think about things that are "excellent," and there is nothing more excellent than a knowledge of Christ. And yet our minds are constantly pulled back and forth from thoughts of Jesus to thoughts of all the things we want outside of Jesus. We become, as it says in James 1:8, a double-minded, unstable woman.

I've seen this in my own life. My thoughts fluctuate from wanting to follow Christ to wanting what I want, and I become unsettled. Contradiction pulls at my mind that sometimes lasts for a moment and sometimes for a season, but while it is present, it is proof of the power that our thoughts have on our souls. We cannot move forward to Christ when our minds are flipping back and forth between what we know is good and what, in the moment, we wish was good. The duality leaves us unbalanced and ineffective, stuck in a very murky understanding of Christ's love.

The remedy is to work at, strain toward, and pray for singleness of mind. Actively pursue a mind focused on Christ. Like Dan, move from intellectual assent to life-altering knowledge of Christ. Speak to yourself the truths about God. Remind yourself that He is omnipotent and humble; empowering and longsuffering; holy and gentle; high in Heaven and near the brokenhearted.

He is excellent and worthy of your thoughts. Cultivate your knowledge of Christ, and your singleness of mind will grow strong within your understanding of His worth. You will suffer the loss of lesser things, and you will win the One who died that you might know Him.

Reflection:

What things do I crave more than Christ?

What are some attributes of God's character that I can think about to help me grasp His immeasurable worth?

Prayer:

Lord, help me to push my thoughts past the desirable, yet broken, things of this world to You, in all your excellence and goodness, and allow a singleness of mind to grow as my thoughts rest more readily on You. In Jesus' name, amen.

25. Praise Him When It Hurts

by Teresa Davis

"And provide for those who grieve in Zion- to bestow on them a crown of beauty instead of ashes, the oil of joy instead of mourning, and a garment of praise instead of a spirit of despair. They will be called oaks of righteousness, a planting of the Lord for the display of his splendor." Isaiah 61:3 (NIV)

It's difficult to take advice from someone who hasn't experienced what they are trying to teach us about. Experience brings credibility, would you agree?

Often we look at Bible heroes as not being human, but this couldn't be further from the truth. Paul had been groomed by the most important man in the Sanhedrin court, Gamaliel. He was a Roman citizen by birth, but was born into a Jewish family. This gave him special rights and influenced his upbringing to follow in Gamaliel's footsteps. His life took a 180° turn on the road to Damascus. This is a perfect example of peripety-a sudden and unexpected change of fortune or reversal of circumstances. He was never meant to be a follower of the "Way." But God had other plans, and we know that what the Lord God Almighty has planned will come to be. "Surely, as I have purposed, so it will be and as I have purposed, so it will happen." Isaiah 14:24

Paul was in prison when he penned four books of the New Testament, including Philippians. He wrote this letter with a spirit of gratitude to thank the people of Philippi for their support. In chapter 4, which is where we find this devotional's key verse, he was teaching us how to have an abundant life, a spirit of joy even when life doesn't turn out like we thought it would. Paul was sitting in a Roman prison encouraging people when he could have been overcome by his thoughts and his present situation.

Our circumstances have the potential to consume our thoughts. How do we have an abundant life in the midst of hard times? What is the secret of being content? When life strips away the most precious to us, it leaves behind what is in our heart and soul. What is in your heart and soul today? Paul said the secret to being content is Jesus. What action are you going to take today to change your thoughts?

The single most decisive action that changed my life after the death of my son was Praise. It feels counterintuitive to be thankful, not for his death, but for the things I still have in my life. Yet, when I praise Him, when I sing with all that is within me, praising Him with tears streaming down my face, it changes my thoughts. For He knows I am weak. Therefore He knows I'm praising Him when my heart hurts and this brings the presence of the Holy Spirit rushing in to comfort me.

When your actions change your thoughts/heart will change. He will give you a garment of praise instead of a spirit of despair. Let me be clear here. If your heart is broken, it will not heal overnight. But when we praise Him and speak aloud what we still have in our life as blessings we will become oaks of righteousness. This mending process only happens with Jesus, and when we praise Him in spite of our circumstances, supernatural power comes into our lives that we simply cannot explain.

Reflection:

How do I have an abundant life in the midst of hard times? What action will I take today to change my thoughts?

Prayer:

Lord Jesus, give me the strength to praise You in the storm. Help me to feel the presence of the Holy Spirit flooding me with comfort. For I know Your word says Your power works best in my weakness. Show me that because of Your strength in my weakness I will become an oak of righteousness that has been planted by the Lord Himself for the display of His splendor. In Jesus' name, amen.

26. Joyous Praise

by Angie Baughman

"Consider it all joy, my brothers *and sisters*, when you encounter various trials." James 1:2 (NASB)

I recently experienced an offer of professional support. I felt God encouraging me to say yes to the collaboration, and I accepted the role. Then I began looking forward to how the experience would grow me and my ministry.

The position did grow me and my ministry. But it did not create growth in the way I had hoped or anticipated. I thought the partnership would mean my message would reach more people. Instead, the work promised to me didn't come to fruition, and the space in which I'd believed I would be elevated and appreciated became a space in which I felt overlooked and set aside.

In those weeks of confusion, I asked God the questions we all ask Him when we take steps in obedience only to be met with a reality far different than our expectations.

"Did I hear You wrong, God?"

"Did You forget about me, God?"

And, ultimately, "Are You still praiseworthy, God?"

As I raised my questions to Him, God began to open my heart again to His relentless desire for me to see myself the way He sees me. For a long time, I have proven myself valuable through productivity, and I consistently rely on my abilities to achieve, organize, and lead to demonstrate my worth.

But in this situation, the productivity-based opportunities that have always been present for me before in professional arenas were absent. I had to decide if I would try to break doors down so I could be let in to shine, or if I would believe that my value came from somewhere much greater. Would I place my trust in the irrevocable promise that I am a child of God (John 1:12) – a promise that has no dependence on my productivity?

The word for joy in James 1:2 that tells us to count it joy when we face trials is the same word used for joy in Matthew 2:10 when the wise men rejoice when they again see the star stopped over the place where they would finally find Jesus. Those two verses are forever connected for me because we, too, sometimes lose sight of the star when we find ourselves in a storm of pain and confusion.

But, like the wise men, when we find Jesus and realize His presence is close to us, we can rejoice and offer praise because we know where Jesus can be found.

I found reason to praise Jesus in my professional disappointment because I recognized He was with me. I praised Him for the loving ways He received my questions. I praised Him for the way He wanted to grow my dependence on Him instead of on myself and the approval of others. I praised Him because He is praiseworthy, and in knowing that truth, there is joy.

Reflection:

Whatever I am facing today, Jesus is here with me. That is reason to praise Him.

Prayer:

Loving God, You are at work in every area of my life. I so quickly stop praising You when something doesn't go my way instead of looking for where You are teaching me something new. Thank You for the many ways You reveal Yourself to me. Help me see You and trust that You are always good. In Jesus' name, amen.

27. What Do You See?

by Sandi Baete

"Be still and know that I am God." Psalm 46:10 (NIV)

One afternoon, my husband and I were looking out our back door and discussing something. I don't remember details, but most likely we were contemplating installing a pool and trying to figure out how many trees would need to be removed for that to happen. We still don't have a pool, so it is just as likely we were discussing how much dog poop our two Brittany Spaniels, Sugar and Cane, had left in our yard. Anyway, there is something much more important I do remember from that conversation.

We were intently focused on our backyard, and just a few minutes into the discussion, when we both noticed animals. Not the dogs, although they were there. First a cardinal, then a blue jay, followed by a squirrel. The longer we watched the more we saw. It was as if our backyard had become a wildlife sanctuary for small creatures. What had really happened is that we had stood still long enough to see what was there. Psalm 46:10 tells us, "Be still and know that I am God." Being still gave us a glimpse of God's creation. Our backyard had truly become a sanctuary where we could praise Him for the beauty of nature.

It made me wonder what other praiseworthy things I was missing in my life. Was busyness blinding me to the goodness all around me? Even though my life is now much simpler in many ways than it has ever been, I can tell you, I often miss many of the praiseworthy things. Too many times in what I would call "being still", my mind is still being entertained or distracted. Our lives are filled with multi-tasking and thinking of what's next, instead of being fully engaged in the moment, the activity, or the conversation we are currently involved in. It's not easy to slow down and take notice, but the more we practice focusing on what's right in front of us, the easier it becomes.

A simple way to do this is to begin to look at the finer details. For example, my husband recently brought flowers to me, and they have been in the center of the kitchen table where I can see them every day. When I sat down to write this piece, I moved them to make room for my laptop, and they caught my eye in a new way. I noticed the intricacies of each type of flower- the colors, textures, and so many other tiny details- that made me appreciate them even more. What do you see every day that you can focus on for a few minutes and find added details about- new things to give praise for?

We know the Lord is praiseworthy for so many reasons. If we were writing a list, providing for our salvation and creating the world we live in would be right at the top. Apart from God, does anything else qualify as praiseworthy? We often think of praiseworthy as being exclusively about God, but what about the co-worker who does an exceptional job on a project, or the friend who calmly, and with love, responds to a social media attack, or the single mom who is patient with her children even when she is exhausted? Are those things not worthy of praise? In Christian terms, we often think of praise as the songs we sing at church. But in the examples above, a simple "Great job!" or "You handled that so well." or "You are a wonderful mom!" would be appropriate ways to give praise for a praiseworthy act. Proverbs 3:27 says, "Do not withhold good from those to whom it is due, when it is in your power to act." God is praiseworthy because He is God, but those around us often behave in a way that is also worthy of praise. Praise we can give without taking away from anything belonging to the Lord.

Reflection:

How can I slow down so I am able to notice the good and the praiseworthy right in front of me?

Make time this week to notice, and acknowledge, a praiseworthy act by a family member, co-worker, or friend.

Prayer:

Lord, may I never withhold praise from You or anyone else. There are reasons every day to praise You, as well as others. Help me to see all the praiseworthy things right in front of me. In Jesus' name, amen.

28. Why We Break a Pattern

by Katie Mason

"Do not conform any longer to the pattern of this world, but be transformed by the renewing of your mind. Then you will be able to test and approve what God's will is—his good, pleasing and perfect will." Romans 12:2 (NIV)

When I was a kid, there was a lot of upheaval in my life. I had two parents who worked full-time. I had three siblings in my house and another house with two more. There were shift changes and mandatory breaks that I had to navigate between. There were different expectations based on what home I was staying at. My family of origin was loud and sometimes chaotic, but I was a quiet kid who longed for structure and order. Or maybe I longed for it because I could never find it? Either way, I developed into a very strong type-A adult who always had a routine, a plan, and a structure that would ensure chaos be kept at bay. This pattern took me through high school, college, and the early years of parenting well. I was seen as a leader, organized, and efficient. I thrived on that praise.

My young family moved a bunch, I had postpartum depression, and my oldest kid was at the doctor's office or hospital more than he was at home. As much as I tried to keep things together, it wasn't working. I needed a new pattern, a new way of going through life. I needed Jesus to transform my mind from one of control to one of surrender to Him.

It took me a while to realize that the chaos I had found myself in was the beginning of God rewiring the thought patterns of both my soul and mind. When I began to see that I couldn't handle things, I turned to the One with hands big enough to carry my load. I opened up my heart and mind to the possibility and hope that what I had been believing was my burden to bear, was actually already being carried by Jesus. My mind needed to be renewed so that I could understand who God was to me.

Sister, we all have places in our minds that are clouded by either half-truths or utter lies. We need to know how to discern what is God's good will for us and what is a distraction from the enemy. Only when we can do that will we be able to walk under the banner of Christ in the full awareness of being called His daughters.

It is important that we are able to know what God's "... good, pleasing and perfect will is." Why? Because knowing that is how we can tell the truth from lies. When we surrender in obedience to letting the Holy Spirit transform our thoughts, we become aware of what God calls us. Names like unworthy, failure, screw-up, and disappointment become replaced with worthy, victor, humble, and overcomer.

We must be willing to let our minds be transformed so that we can know what God wants us to do. If our minds are plagued by self-doubt and societal pressure, we cannot believe what we read in God's holy Word. Things like Jeremiah 29:11 which says, "'For I know the plans I have for you,' declares the Lord, 'plans to prosper you and not to harm you, plans to give you hope and a future.'" If we are so focused on how we have been hurt in the past that we cannot see ahead of where we are, how can we believe that truth? If we have been so focused on our cultural drive for success, we cannot see the relief in knowing that "we are God's workmanship, created in Christ Jesus to do good works, which God prepared in advance for us to do." Ephesians 2:10

Friend, know that God the Father made you. He knows you better than even you know yourself. Surrender to His gentle hands and allow Him to transform you. Taste and see that our God is good. Let us walk together in knowing His good, pleasing and perfect will for our lives.

Reflection:

What patterns do I need to let go of?

Where does God need to begin renewing my mind?

Prayer:

Lord Jesus, I pray that You would transform my mind. That You would break the patterns of lies and deception that I have been believing. Holy Spirit, take every thought captive so I can know what is Your Truth. Please help me to walk under Your banner of victory, not my own tattered rags of self-help or experience. Father, I trust in You to show me Your will. Clear my mind of what would make that unclear. In Jesus' name, amen.

29. The Mind is the Battlefield

by Teresa Davis

"We demolish arguments and every pretension that sets itself up against the knowledge of God, and we take captive every thought to make it obedient to Christ." 2 Corinthians 10:5 (NIV)

The battle is won or lost in the mind. Do you agree with that statement? I once interviewed a psychologist who specializes in treating people who are traumatized by war, death, fear, guilt, rape, and other traumas too numerous to mention. He is a person of faith and expressed to me that most Christians think the enemy is out to take away our joy. But his belief was that the enemy's goal was to destroy our minds. I agree!

We may not have control over the thoughts that enter our minds. But! We do have control over what we do with the thoughts. Do we feed them or starve them? How do we conquer the thoughts that rush our minds every day? Paul sets the stage for how serious the battle is. He uses military terms to describe the actions we must take to win, because it is indeed a war. We demolish the thought, take it down, remove it from its pedestal as it lords over us, taunting us with "sophisticated arguments." (AMP) Don't you just love how Paul uses the word "arguments"? This tells me he knows exactly what he is describing because he has felt every bit as tempted as we are.

The thought comes as lofty and proud and exalts itself as the authority over us, attempting to convince us that it is absolute truth regardless of the facts. The enemy is cunning and knows exactly how to tempt us by our own desires. He knows what makes us tick and what our hearts long to have. Therefore, he uses half-truths to convince us to believe the whole thought as absolute truth. Once he has accomplished his goal, we are well on our way to making the thought a reality. How do we stop it? Once we recognize it for what it is, then we must take it captive.

During war, what happens when a prisoner is caught? More often than not, they are taken to a secure place and interrogated. We must interrogate the thought against the knowledge of God's Word- the truth. How do we do that? I have a method I began using after the death of my son. He died suddenly and my world turned upside down. My thoughts looked like a million cars trying to cross an intersection all at the same time. Imagine all the traffic lights blinking at different times and all the cars (my thoughts) trying to push through the light. Total chaos!

As the thoughts came flying through my mind, one after another, I would focus on one. I would take that thought and write it down. It brings clarity when we use more than one sense to examine the thought. After I wrote it down, I would say the thought out loud. Saying the thought out loud had a significant impact on me because sometimes it sounded absurd. As I heard myself say the words out loud I knew immediately that it was not believable. When I needed more clarity, I would rebut the thought with God's Word. Once I determined the thought was a lie, the next time it came I was ready.

I would speak to the thought and tear it apart. I knocked it down, took it off its place of authority, and destroyed it with God's Word.

That is how we win the battle of the mind. When we take thoughts captive and make them stand against our God they will crumble into a million pieces and lose their power over us. When we call on our God for help, He will answer and reveal Himself in ways we couldn't have imagined. "Call to me and I will answer you. I'll tell you marvelous and wondrous things that you could never figure out on your own." Jeremiah 33:3 (MSG)

Reflection:

What's stopping me from taking my thoughts captive? The more I practice the process the more it will become a habit, and I will be able to stop those destructive thoughts in their tracks.

Prayer:

Lord Jesus, reveal to my hurting heart that You are for me not against me. Let me find strength in You. In Jesus' name, amen.

30. Change Your Life

by Cassia Elder

"For as he thinks in his heart, so *is* he." Proverbs 23:7a (NKJV)

You are what you think.

Our key verse for this devotional book, Philippians 4:8, says, "think about these things." Some translations say, "dwell on these things." This interesting word choice emphasizes not just what crosses our minds, but also the way we live.

You see, while the admonition to "think about these things" includes the thoughts that take up space in our brains, it also encompasses so much more.

Romans 8:5-6 (NIV) says, "Those who live according to the flesh have their minds set on what the flesh desires; but those who live in accordance with the Spirit have their minds set on what the Spirit desires. The mind governed by the flesh is death, but the mind governed by the Spirit is life and peace."

The way we live is determined by what we allow to rule in our minds. Our thinking will either be consumed with self or full of the Spirit, and our actions always follow suit. We can walk in one of two ways—the path that leads to destruction or the one that leads to peace.

We not only have the ability to choose our thoughts but, so much more importantly, it is our responsibility to choose well. As a result, we choose the way we live. The choice has been "set before you life and death, blessings and curses. Now choose life." Deuteronomy 30:19b (NIV)

If our minds are dominated by the desires of our flesh, our actions will be self-focused. With no regard for the desires of God or the needs of others, we will make decisions to pursue our own interests and to fulfill our every pleasure.

When our minds are governed by the Spirit, we will live according to the Spirit. As we bring our thoughts into alignment with His thoughts, His will becomes our will. Our aspirations will no longer be to fulfill our own selfish desires. Our attention will become others-focused as we serve God by serving people. The longing of our hearts will shift to accomplishing His good purpose.

Jesus did not come to make us better versions of ourselves. He came to make us new creations so that we continually become less like us and more like Him.

May we submit to the transformative work of the Holy Spirit. Allow His power to penetrate our entire beings so that we not only *think about these things* but also live out these things.

Live true. Live honorable. Live right. Live pure. Live lovely. Live commendable. Live excellent. Live praiseworthy.

When we change our minds, we change our lives.

Reflection:

Are my thoughts being governed by the desires of my flesh or by the will of the Holy Spirit?

How will I intentionally partner with the Holy Spirit to not only *think about these things* but also live out these things?

Prayer:

Father God, I understand that I can choose my thoughts, and what I think directly impacts my actions. I want to choose life but sometimes my flesh gets in the way. Please teach me to submit to the transformative work of Your Holy Spirit. Make me new, not only in the way I think, but, most importantly, in the way I live. Lord, change my thoughts and change my life. In Jesus' name, amen.

Sisters Forward

Contributors

 **Cassia Elder** is an Author, Speaker, and Founder of *Sisters Forward*. She lives in a little log cabin on the creek with her husband Chris, their son Asa, and a porch-sittin' hound dog named Moonshine. She is a nerd for God's Word who has been passionate about crafting with words since joining the Young Author's Club in the fourth grade.

At the heart of every message Cassia shares, you will find the Greatest Commandment in light of the Great Commission. She comes alongside her Sisters in Christ from a place of relationship with the call to live in all that God has for them and live out His purpose in the world. Her vision is to build women up and propel them forward in their walk with Jesus. With a passion to rightly handle the Word, Cassia shares practical application for life today that is firmly rooted in Scripture.

In Cassia's debut book, "Make Me a Blessing," readers discover how "Your Ordinary Life Can Have Eternal Impact." As women have engaged with her message, through her books, Bible studies, and at in-person events, unending ripples of blessing have been created.

Connect with Cassia:
cassiaelder.com
https://linktr.ee/CassiaElder

 *Sheri Trusty* is an award-winning newspaper correspondent, portrait and nature photographer, Sisters Forward Contributor, and owner of Wing Shadow, which features Sheri's written and photographic work. Since 2006, Sheri has worked as a correspondent for two USA Today Network newspapers, where her writing and photography combine into one of her greatest pleasures: promoting the amazing people who live in her community. Sheri's favorite people to applaud with pen and lens are her two grown sons, Pax and Jon. Sheri and her husband, Gary, live in rural Ohio about 30 miles from Sheri's happy place, Lake Erie, on a two-acre plot they keep stocked with peanuts, birdseed, and suet cakes for the dozens of wild birds who also call it home.

Sheri's photography was included in a project that was honored with a James Beard award, and her photos have been featured in restaurants and universities across the country. She finds great joy in capturing the beauty of God's handiwork displayed in His people and the natural world. It is Sheri's hope that her work quietly shouts the incredible love and creativity of the Creator so fully that it inspires others to long for His presence in their lives.

Connect with Sheri:
www.wingshadowphotography.com
https://linktr.ee/sherit44

 *Katie Mason* is a writer, communicator, encourager, and speaker who brings encouragement to others through God's Word. One of her passions is to advocate for the voiceless, marginalized, and broken. She is a co-founder and Coordinator of Midtown MOPS that serves Moms of all ages in the Southern Indiana community. Katie is also the founder and owner of Four Paths: Spiritual Direction Ministry.

Katie is currently doing life with her family on the north side of Louisville. She enjoys suburban life that keeps her close to interesting people and restaurants while keeping mileage low on her car. The Mason Family enjoys playing games, visiting family, and spending time with friends. With a blend of artistic temperaments, there is usually a lively discussion happening somewhere in their home.

Katie enjoys eating good food, drinking a cup of hot tea, reading a great book, and studying the intricacies of God's Word. Katie's musings on life are found on her blog, Facebook page, and through public speaking events. She seeks out opportunities to share and hear stories from the people she meets. She also believes firmly in the power of healing through the sharing of our life stories. Katie is also firmly dedicated to the unity of the church in Christ and its ability to set captives free through the power of God.

Connect with Katie:
https://avoicetocallout.blogspot.com
https://linktr.ee/ktmason21

Angie Baughman is a pastor, author, podcaster, founder of Steady On Ministries, and creator of the Step By Step Bible study method. She is trained in inductive Bible study through Precept ministries, served on Kathi Lipp's ministry team, and is an Academy Mentor for FlourishWriters.

Angie is a trauma and abuse survivor who speaks openly about her ongoing journey towards deeper healing. She loves sipping cups of hot tea, watching medical and crime dramas, planning trips to Walt Disney World, and almost anything with a paisley print.

Steady On is a place to find the personal manifestation of God in the painful places of our lives. The ministry is based on the promise of Psalm 40:2, "He set my feet on solid ground and steadied me as I walked along." (NLT)

Angie lives in Southern Illinois with her husband and two sons.

Connect with Angie directly at angie@livesteadyon.com

Find the latest from Steady On at https://linktr.ee/livesteadyon

 *Sandi Baete* is a wordsmith who loves sharing practical ways of living out the truths of Scripture in everyday life. She has been married to Joe since 1989 and they have three grown children. They love being Bibi and Pa to their precious grandson and are excited to welcome more grandchildren into their lives soon.

Sandi and her husband own Party Central Rental and she founded The Teacher Encouragement Project. Her hobbies include reading, giving meaningful gifts, and having coffee with friends. Her circle is small, but she loves big, calling herself "frugally extravagant."

Sandi's mission in life is to love her husband well, be brave with her gifts and talents so her children will do the same, and in all things to be her Lord's servant. She is honored to be a *Sisters Forward* contributor and hopes you will connect with her on Facebook at:

https://www.facebook.com/kaleidoscoperemnant
or by scanning the QR code below.

 *Teresa Davis* is an encourager by design and has helped many on their journey toward healing. She considers herself to be a temporary traveler in a broken world, longing for home. Teresa's purpose is to help others see Jesus in the worst this world has to offer. She writes, "As long as I draw breath, I will strive to bring glory to His name. Heaven is more real to me than ever before, because one of my children lives there." The eyes of grief sent her on a quest to see if she believed God was who He said He was. The lens she now views life from has transformed her heart and mind. She now professes to love Jesus more than she ever thought possible.

Teresa encourages and challenges audiences to see life through a different lens when the unexpected comes knocking at their door. Through God's word she will equip the reader to take the next step with Jesus even when it hurts. Finding Hope and Healing in the Midst of Grief is a devotion Teresa authored after the death of her son.

To those who know her best she loves with her whole heart and sees each day as a gift. A wife of 39 years, mother of two and Nana to five grand babies. As a practicing RN she has spent her life serving those in need. Her life verse is found in 1 Peter 4:8 "Above all else love each other deeply."

Connect with Teresa:
www.thegriefmentor.com
https://linktr.ee/Thegriefmentor

 ***Stephanie Heitz*** is a lover of people and considers it pure joy to turn strangers quickly into friends. She enjoys using her voice to make music for the Lord, and pour encouragement into others. Stephanie has been releasing original music on streaming platforms since 2019 with the ultimate goal of encouraging and inspiring her listeners.

Inspired by her jazz musician grandmother, many of Stephanie's earliest childhood memories involve sitting beside her grandma "Mimi" on the piano bench harmonizing to classic tunes. Stephanie is passionate about ministering to others through singing. She serves as a worship leader at a multicultural church in the south end of Louisville, Kentucky. You can also find her speaking, as well as leading worship for women's retreats, New Albany Community Bible Study, and special events throughout the region.

Born and raised in southern Indiana, Stephanie resides in Floyd's Knobs, Indiana with her husband, and several of their five children who are one by one beginning to leave the nest. She enjoys spending time with her family, going on dates with her husband, baking healthy treats, flea marketing for treasures, and creating original songs on her ukulele & keyboard. However, Stephanie is most enthusiastic every day about simply loving people like Jesus.

Music on Spotify and
all major streaming platforms.
@stephanieheitzmusic

Lindsey Hartlage is a wife, homeschool mom, friend, and editor for the Sisters Forward books. She enjoys drinking coffee and having long conversations while wearing her favorite sweatshirts. You can find her traipsing through the woods with her husband and two spirited sons, or imitating the Swedish Chef while cooking up her favorite dishes in her kitchen. Her love of trying new dishes is rivaled only by her love of the Oxford comma.

Mission Partner
Forget Me Not Ministries

Forget Me Not Ministries is a Christian non-profit that strives to educate, equip, and empower at-risk Roma gypsies to prevent abandonment, abuse, trafficking, and child marriages in Romania.

Their vision is to connect the Roma to Christ through community development programs and protection from injustice, so they may live in the love, mercy, and freedom that God has for them. Three ways to give:

Empowerment through Employment - FMN creates days of work for Roma families facing an overwhelming 90% unemployment due to discrimination and lack of education. Sponsor a day of work for a family, provide transportation, and a warm meal for $30.
https://tinyurl.com/FMNjobs

Teen sponsorship - FMN teens are rescued girls who have been sold and recovered. Protect them from trafficking by providing days of employment, education, a refuge shelter, warm meals, and spiritual discipleship for $30 monthly. https://tinyurl.com/FMNteens

Child sponsorship – Break the cycle of abandonment by providing for the Roma and at-risk children. Sponsor a child to provide for their medical needs, education, clothing, food, and spiritual growth.
https://tinyurl.com/FMNchild

Also available from
Sisters Forward

Fruit Full
Devotional

Sisters Forward Journal

NOW AVAILABLE on Amazon!

Bring
Sisters Forward
GATHERING
to your church!

Sisters Forward is a life-changing, in-person women's ministry event.

We partner with local churches to bring this faith-filled half-day event to your community.

SISTERS FORWARD GATHERING FEATURES:

Powerful Live Worship

Practical Bible Teaching from our Dynamic Team of Speakers

Community Engagement with the Host Church

Mission Partners Doing Kingdom Work Locally & Globally

For more info email:
connect@cassiaelder.com

www.ingramcontent.com/pod-product-compliance
Lightning Source LLC
Chambersburg PA
CBHW070854050426
42453CB00012B/2195